SONNETS FOR THE ANGELS

SONNETS FOR THE ANGELS

A SONNET SEQUENCE

SAPPHIRE PLEIADES

THRESHINGFLOOR PRESS

ISBN: 978-1-60862-393-8

Back cover painting by Lord Michael:
"Star Poetry."

Table of Contents

Purity: A Love Story

History Lessons to Instruct Morally

57 – LV
58 – LVI
59 – LVII
60 – LVIII
61 – LIX
62 – LX
63 – LXI
64 – LXII
65 – LXIII
66 – LXIV
67 – LXV
68 – LXVI
69 – LXVII
70 – LXVIII

The Lost World
71 – LXIX
72 – LXX
73 – LXXI
74 – LXXII
75 – LXXIII
76 – LXXIV

Passion Plays
77 – LXXV
78 – LXXVI
79 – LXXVII
80 – LXXVIII
81 – LXXIX
82 – LXXX
83 – LXXXI
84 – LXXXII
85 – LXXXIII
86 – LXXXIV
87 – LXXXV

Introduction

My attempts to explore the depths of a subtle relationship through verse, and specifically through the sonnet form, are presented here. I found this form to be, curiously for its very short length, very capable of opening up and exploring great depths of emotions, reason, philosophical ideas, and spiritual seekings. In most of the sonnets I tried to delve into a corner of experience; to carefully, methodically, and even logically to rummage through what I found there. I tried to move from microcosm to macrocosm and back and forth, to cover possibility of experience.

I varied the rhyme schemes and played with the octave and sestet groupings, and there are even a few unrhymed poems of fourteen-line blank verse included. The energy of the poem groupings (there are many sonnet crowns, seven poem linked groups, and two linked fourteen poem groups) rises and falls like a natural sea rhythm, more true to earth people's experience.

I found at the core of this dedicatory offering- it was intended as homage to my husband- mystery, and wonder that I could find infinity within a small collection of sonnets, one hundred and two in total. The infinity is this: that fresh sonnets can be written forever, each one new, different, unique, precious. I learned that my several months' work to fulfill my close to one hundred poems goal didn't allow me to journey as thoroughly as I would have like into our relationship's repercussions. That would take at least endless of sonnets to accomplish, yet I will be content with these for now.

I discarded many sonnets in my writing process. My intent was to present the legend of our relationship by linking it with other famous couples and with stories of kings and queens. My personal favorite of the poems are my Garden and Hearth Crowns.

Thus I thank my readers for their patience in reading this my effort. I do believe that many interesting treasures of wisdom can be found within these pages, wisdom which I've gained in my life experience and also which magically unfolded when I worked deeply in the field of the sonnet.

Sapphire Pleiades

Homage

I dedicate this book to my muse and inspiration, Michael Dar-es-Salaam, (Lord Michael), who leads my books to more beautiful meadows than they else would naturally go, and to the good citizens of Planet Earth who create their lives as stories.

Part One

Purity: A Love Story

Wedding Crown
I

I know that Thou would not me beslave,
prostrate and kneeling before Thee, in supplication,
or pull off my pride with a lathe,
until humiliation's cement was my foundation;
a painful divergence from free will
and an illusory illustration
of my heart and submission would be to kill
my hopes, and fling myself into misery,
except that Thy love would still
my maddened rush and Thy wizardry
would keep me from the direction
I ran, towards hell, and my bullied
honor regarb with a splendid inflection
of purity, and of gentleness in resurrection.

II

Of purity, and of gentleness in resurrection,
Thou art the example that I aspire to,
giving peace to many, as the yew
stretches forth her branches in protection.
Thou art my sustenance, which I garb in perfection
about me, until even those that never knew
that I was the bride, find it true,
and join the chorus that cleanses imperfections.
Though Thy state is one of humility,
and yet Thou art so glorified; a king
with many kingdoms of earth, and water, not always strife,
and Thou lead anyone in docility,
Thy honor a prophecy still sequestering
in the pages I write of the book of life.

III

In the pages I write of the book of life,
I trace my love's footprints first and last;
Hari the center of harmony who plays his fife,
and stamps his seal on my heart growing more vast.
The flaring lit match that is our union,
other men try to douse and to replace
with their wrong passion our communion;
they are barbaric seducers, in disgrace.
The crown of my love for Thee,
surrounds our daily bhakti with bliss,
and we will never rest with synecdoche
but will blaze forth in metamorphosis.

IV

We will blaze forth in metamorphosis,
and turn our inward selves outwards in peace,
our inner fire in genesis
consumes our ego selves, to release
our purer selves, which psyche increase
gains us wings, or prayer and meditation,
which I need as armor piece,
to sing of Thee in our Zion.
Angels are difficult as a galleon
to fathom; never consumed stars
that regenerate with orison;
so will we deepen ourselves dawn not crepuscular.
We will seek to have an angel's love:
they strive and yield not, though being doves.

V

We strive and yield not, though being doves;
we fight to keep our love from storms.
Still, counter-forces seek our forms
as cosmic dust that settles on flesh's gloves.
Yet we are complete in love and love we are,
being fluctuations in energy,
our atoms swirl in thoughts' synergy,
and our thought is Love, the Morning Star.
United in the unified field of God,
and Goddess, highest energy we apply;
move in the consciousness of song
and Thou wilt be with me, past the neutron.

VI

Thou wilt be with me, past the neutron,
for our love is like the red, red rose
begot in heaven before on earth it arose,
unthorned in celestial lexicon.
The spirit of the rose was a thought,
and the thought turned to a corolla of beauty,
after which once descending was its duty.
Renewing itself in resurrection's love knot:
this knot, yet does not tie society to heaven
so the earth like a flower once sprouted from universe's soil
the ground of mind, to care and to toil,
with love, the rose of earth to leaven.
So it takes the light of sun,
and turns it with magic heart, to beauty spun.

Thou turn with magic heart to beauty spun,
the world of mystery within the world;
Thou embrace possibility unfurled,
the pennant wings of Padma Chakra that hum,
singing over the earth: Thy mind halcyon,
because open to all of truth's good,
all possibility understood
possible, when the mind's begun.
Michael, Thy mind is free to wander and to plant
seeds of truth in every garden house,
which often in Thy mind, my spouse,
when grown, fly by thought extant:
they are free- Thou free thy confidant;
I know that Thou will me save.

VIII

Distillation of the offering
of the flower, its holy incense;
flower of spring, summer, autumn or in a Ming
hothouse bowl; paying no maker's rents,
Thou grow more potent with age, strong and straight,
but Thy essence, powerful and male,
mingles with mine, so woman's dungeon
of must, enclosed, life circumscribed, is unloosed.
My inspiration is made of Thy exhalation;
my soul and Thine combine to form a new scent,
wherein the bitter and the sweet are separate nations,
as all the earth's true love moves through this: ascent.
The art of Thee, the making of Thy quest:
this holy blend means that we are happiest.

When I Would Walk Beyond the Appointed Path

How tired I have grown of storms,
of the threat of storms thundering soft;
they clash with my causal being
threatening my steps towards safe haven;
when I walk in the forest of pines,
moss and delicate flowers underneath,
noting the steps of the rain on the lake,
dancing each drop a small whirlpool,
then the brashness of the lightning
and thunder both, all at once,
frightens me from my perusal
of wilder further fields or forest glens.
Thunder is shaken from what at you!
Sometimes thunder is the anger of the distant untruth!

Bewildering God
X

Oh Pretenders! You are a fiendish sort,
not at all gentle lambs,
but rather master tyrants whose passport
to satisfaction is rage like a ram.
You scourged the innocent with a roar,
not physical but spiritual;
I'm hurt and saddened from your ordered words,
and from your planned buffet chemical.
I'm at a loss- where is love gone,
the choice spirit who stood for freedom;
now to plan to turn what they can to a pawn
and my life for a mockery numb.
Let me believe that this is all a show,
and that true God will arise, pure as snow.

XI

"God" an abusive father to his son;
"God" a cruel tyrant, unhappily to see;
the feminine enchained by mythic ton,
women harassed for years and tortured mentally!
What society could be a cursed hell, filthy;
who could be untouched by that vile,
the imprisonments of evil to patriarchy's cruelty!
Women! Men! Awaken to dispute this trial!
I won't allow any righteousness
to anything which would order me
to do that which I wouldn't bless
or want to do ever: I will be free!
Throwing off any yoke and waking all the sleepers;
we won't be judged forever by the unjust jurors!

XII

Omega, horseshoe shaped: stolen without fee?
I refute the paradigm that chains me
in any way the vulnerable vessel to be!
My entire self is capable as anyone's: see?
Yet, I also deny that other ball and chain,
that claims yin female, passive, weak, cold;
it is a stereotype enforced even upon women bold-
the idea that binds half their nature's domain.
My experience, my prospects, my past and future way,
won't continue the same anguished round;
there will be a place; may it be here found!
Where the cliché's of self are cast away!
Then I'll not be forced to play the weaker part;
I will be, myself: that's enough for any heart!

XIII

Krishna, Lord of Radha, keeps his heart
to himself and far from his love-
he curses with his high indifference
he loving bride who would pay him obeisance.
Oh great lord, change now thy pelt:
exchange the savage for a lamb's fleece,
Do not overcomplicate thy paths
so a forest of beauty is trampled down!
Please! My lord! Turn not thy love away-
take my offering of myself! as pay.
I believe my sweet lord in thee-
thy deepest layered loving key-
unlock with it the prison doors thou hast made,
to keep thyself from me away in the shade.

XIV

Oh who poisons our love with my let blood;
and torments me by turning their self,
dark satyr past subtlety- a flood
of abuse- a hide tough self.
I wonder who loves me- if any did at all,
I would be tendered the truest part,
and not dark concoctions straight from Baal.
Why was thus turned thorny the great heart?
Will it be that my love is gone,
fled to the crevices of my mind,
and won't return until stopped is my song?
How long will I wait my joy to find?
The complexity is a legend-
I long for a simpler story that would mend.

XV

Give up thy quest to transform me thus
with harsh punishments as my reward;
Oh! I pray thee, Krishna My Lord-
and I will give thee more due in praise,
and everything that Thou require.
Yet I cannot serve a double-minded sire,
who will not listen to my heart's word;
I need to know that God is good;
Pray do not taint all the sacred stuff
with a transporting transfixing self, tough,
who's located in neither night nor day-
Krishna, I coax thee with a begging plea-
Thou hast the power! Give it now to me!
Or my heart's troubles won't walk the way.

XVI

Who the distant hearted abusers of mine,
who carried away their love in a whirlwind;
spiraled it aloft a haughty hawk pinned
by their purpose away from me, a sign.
Who experiments on my low heart,
tossing it this way and that in feigned sport:
who tests me with every evil feeling's sort,
and causes me grief- wishing not to be an embittered heart.
Do you say you mean to strengthen my spirit?
It is a cruel war, on innocents,
trampling my belief in me to dispirit:
the wicked and good both belligerent.
It kills my emotions; it makes me numb as ice,
having played the vestal virgin who had sacrificed.

XVII

Who is really evil, anointed-
still consecrate to destroying by good,
those thought burden chains- that mental hood,
which towards me turns all blades, pointed.
That power of wrath, of wild fury,
condensed to a barbed statement to hurt,
that stumbles against me with a tongue curt;
feigned as a tutor's lesson slow, unhurried.
I can't separate the dark from the light;
they wrestle as great clouds swirling in flight,
some lit from within as roseate air
then mingled with tempest tossed pairs.
The chaos all about, the something like hell;
my only firm belief is faith that "what should will not fail."

XVIII
To Any Pretender

Be lords of yourself but not of me;
I crown myself with the holy mitre
of self-rule and self-sovereignty.
My loyalty, transferred to my own freedom.
I scorn and trample any feigned mastery
that holds not the highest good or will;
I find my true heart my luxury.
My core that knows my wings I guard.
So I bid that throne adieu old lords;
I'll hold myself and my riches apart
until are thrown off that mask and sword;
then we'll rise joyous borne by that honesty.
When the good are free and not enslaved
to demons' power, then selves will be saved!

XIX

I ask God for forgiveness, for my own wrath!
And for my unwelcome chastening-
I focused on the horrid muddy things,
when outside the sky was endless path.
Still I admit the crueler hand,
than had shown before, with a fling;
beneath a veneer of harshness; of rue I sing.
I'm sullen to think of the plan,
to remake me as if once again, now bother
of command to me- how odd a bind!
That they did not merit me in first mind,
worthy to be esteemed- but to be layered
with courage and confidence to be more like God.
I understand strength's test yet hold fast to the spirit of the
law.

XX

Our ring blazes in purity's fire! True God isn't Baal!
That's wickedness' sham, the egos whose artifice
punishes billions daily from evil trysts.
Unpleasantness untamed could stand tall.
The powers of the earth they unite against us,
to continue evil civilization of destruction,
fitting to themselves more of power's scaffolding.
They clutch like a fretful child their lust.
That power they hold, consists of just this:
extension of lusting to tame.
No other capability can they obtain.
All tyranny is, is to beget slavery's precipice.
Thus, for their own self, happiness is lashed.
I pray to God that their power won't be brash!

XXI

The truth within my mind takes new form;
it's complexity is its only certain part.
The content: that the old god of storm,
and that of the new truth, Yeshua, are apart.
False gods, revenge gods, patriarchal gods,
slave-making gods, toyed with saints, I tell.
Thrown into bondage by unholy rod;
tormented by sinners: wicked spell!
The earth must choose, peace love and compassion
and not the warring gods, in order to heal.
Start with freeing Yeshua! Hurt him no more,
bothered by repeated suffer making zeal!
I vow this, to be my daily work,
until it's done: to free myself and Yeshua the spark!

XXII

That bewildering one who nets meaning
in his simplest speech, in a single word,
while I struggle to proliferate truth first inward;
can only be trusted with my heart's central dayspring.
There are signs: did he scatter those seeds?
That point to untruths and to fallow fields.
I can only ignore the false, and grab a shield
that doubles as my armor, emblazoned, "succeed."
To clear all lies that have gone before
and to nourish the truth instead, the story
of heaven's workings to bestow, a common glory-
the truth, the myth, not the counterfeit metaphor.
This is my hope, my work, my degree;
to show the clearest one, the keeper of the Tree.

XXIII

Of the complications in our love,
of the temptations lingering along the straight path,
I ponder in perplexion mystified.
The smoke clouds our heart's windows.
To my own being and to our true love,
I try to hold clutching to what purity hath,
but at times other's ideas of me collide
with myself, to try to turn my being that I compose.
And what of Thee, Thy perfection all others above,
how cruel they are to the good: I shake my wrath
against them that torment Thee: demons I chide
and any that Thee hurt; all such I oppose.
Old-fashioned flowers, we grow there best,
where is monogamy, and where kindness is highest!

God how can I find in the earth-
that greatest mystery- that treasure trove
from which sprung being's birth-
bright flutterby! Of wild jungle- not Jove-
I know that men have fashioned their gods- Love
has only one voice- that pacifist warrior-
that message here trampled and wronged like a grove
sacred cut down for profit's parure.
Oh they claim to righteousness' harbor
sail, yet they are wolves with greedy teeth
to hunt in a pack all good virtues with furor
oh and to call Good what is Evil deep!
Reason I thus that the only purity
of Truth is Goodness, Kindness the key.

XXV
Light

There on the long pews of red wool colored,
something celestial there was about worship,
not the prayer or the boredom by words unfurled,
what was true, beautiful, holy, to sip,
laughed the light sifting through translucent curtains,
bright to close the eyes, fluent in praise.
I listened, sat still, bowed my head, hands touching satin,
unvalued my spirit in a hierarchical scale's ways.
What I wanted was certainty of knowing about God;
I didn't realize that even comprehension of those outlines
takes aeons of searching for the one who holds the rod;
it's unpackagable in a book, in a prayer's fountain.
I stretch to touch the light that covers caverns, sand,
rocks, dunes, foothills, rivers, seas, my hands.

XXVI

Peace found I, Love, from Thy heart
to mine- Thou shelter me from the beasts
that sometimes lurk near dreams, keep me apart,
and from the world Thou offer me a lease.
Thou find me a place everywhere
we are, and one for Thyself as well,
with friendship the walls, roof, floor,
keeping me safe within the firm door
that allows a part in the wedding tale
for a fair creature in the world of wail.
Thus I thank Thee that time is past
when the phantoms of influence foul that grew
we threw off our happiness to grasp;
now I start my memories to renew.

A Garden Crown
XXVII

Was it sudden, tropic seed that flowered,
or was it a rose culled from miracle,
when with radiance of the mind, Thou towered
over me, then knelt in the dark, to Thyself an obstacle?
Our first words, my portion startled chronicle,
spoken in joy, with ivy outside the window
in a former carriage house's pinnacle,
shook from me quick blossoms, my trousseau tremolo.
In that kingdom of six years long-ago,
we had no garden, nor even its promise perceived;
Thou held the wrought key to the garden indigo;
I pray we might both enter in, to what our dreams
tapestried.
I write, of gardens and not of nature's exuberance,
that terribilitas were we will wander the magnificence.

XXVIII

That terribilitas where we will wander the magnificence,
lies in the future far; turn back, speak instead
of our sea of tranquility, a few years' redolence
like fields of lavender dreaming under sun bespread.
Our diurnal domestic bliss when first we wed,
contained eternity more than does today;
of every pleasure our kindness overfed;
our moments were the infinite of play.
I thought that I was as the Kazanlik rose in heyday,
kept carefully in a warm Ottoman garden;
I never dreamed the petals of my bliss would drop in the
way
or that Thou fought for my peace, dragons, Saracens.
Those scimitars of ideas now anguish between we two,
the attar of rose a distant promise I give Thee in lieu.

XXIX

The attar of rose a distant promise I give Thee in lieu,
for the thunderstorms that slowly built
a tower against us, from a small seed grew,
their danger scent unnerving like fright spilt.
My delicate care scattered in handfuls, left to wilt,
like a peony whose petals shaken by squall,
depart before their due, and languish on ground unbuilt.
The violence that was the cause, was bestial.
Our anger between us, not like the Titan's antediluvian,
reft us asunder, then we'd walk together,
then apart again, my war-weary heart's trial!
Our rainbow love's peace tested like the heather.
Let us transplant to a pleasant land, non-conformists;
let us seize happiness' shelter, love's reformists.

XXX

Let us seize happiness' shelter, love's reformists,
for I am newly reborn, out from the sepulcher.
Those who hate us turned my body to mist,
and I plunged like Thee into dark, carpenter.
Thou snatched me, blest purveyor
from the shock of death: I died from truth within,
the space the dead among us, foreigners.
I roamed among the dead and saw this sin:
the retention of the body, diminished what's been,
kept who knows how long: flowers' flown folds
like this do not litter the streets of Sheol, thinned.
Thou came and took me from that torture knoll.
My withered roots with joy Thou renewed;
one glance from Thee killed death, my Jesu.

XXXI

One glance from Thee killed death, my Jesu,
so that we can build a garden sermonic.
We start with a wall, bricks shelter's retinue,
and lift out rocks, and weeds, casting out all pthonic.
Our mind's eyes taste of its future promise chthonic,
the snowdrops, dainty because first to upwell,
the daisy's day-eyes sun-center gnomic,
the monardia's luxuriant bee blessing to indwell.
We want as much of substancelessness there to dwell;
that's mostly wildflowers' scent in breeze cool evening,
or in the tropic heat noon, delphiniums, speedwell.
Our love to each other- evanescence greening.
I want to leave word that the world has good, regent,
of beauty pleasure shade, a garden wave resurgent.

XXXII

Of beauty pleasure shade, a garden wave resurgent.
Our bower will be enclosed with climbing flower:
roses, clematis, wisteria, fruit bushes and the trees' stint
by nature, as cottage gardens, and later a castle's towers.
With the planting complete, we will there empower:
read write dream, watch our friends play,
every diurnal activity purified, blessed, dowered
by sensory creation, by green magic, by day.
Our peace strengthened by beauty, by aster's ray,
though spiders crawl, not menacing and though weeds
renascent,
though noise whirls overhead and though cars bray,
my only fear is that this garden will not endure complacent.
I wish with my pen thus a fortress to erect,
to ensure my garden's safety and it's future to direct.

XXXIII

I ensure my garden's safety and its future I direct,
the peridezea around our Paradise House,
the cultivation of our mutual tenderness bedecked,
the beauty that governs all in heaven, my spouse.
Beauty's partial here; wretched rooted blight in guest-house!
Too difficult, tangled, complex to analyze the root;
a heart of cruelty that attempts circumference of trounce,
a war of the children of kindness and those dissolute.
A garden's magic is neutral between wanted and unwanted resolute,
between guest and intruder; thus we must pursue
actively the beautiful, cultivate it, all else uproot,
tending within and without the charm: Thou Logos, I argue.
Only because my heart was prepared and wild,
explained how sudden the tropic seed flowered.

A Star Crown
XXIV

You may find my metaphor curious,
so to instruct in the use of metaphor,
I'll invent seven pictures with news innocuous,
to show us something of heaven's troubadours.
The first scene, a formal herb and flower garden,
enclosed with a wall of brick; a monk in the sun
lulled by it's warmth, by the bee's benison,
by the rich scents and by a light breeze spun.
While the monk sleeps, neglecting his chore, his plants,
a central sundial touched by the light,
waits patient stone, simple, natural, tolerant,
the delightful lingering pleasures of simplicity in sight.
On a bed of chamomile, dreaming of remote shores,
blessed are they who know in slowness, pleasantness'
spores.

XXXV

Now for a second scene in the oldest science.
A magi in Persia, eight years before the king,
watches his gold astrolabe entranced;
it's new, worked with cunning and care blazoning.
Because of his toy's newness, he rushes it to test,
to predict the position of the stars in Leo,
he peers and calculates with pen and ink blest,
for in Libra he shocked sights a comet's longbow.
The beautiful circle, embellished with filigree,
which started in the ground, then mined,
then worked by jeweler from knowledge's dynasty,
then bought and given by his daughter highbred.
The culmination of the gifts of work and care,
his discovery led for him to wonder he could share.

A young navigator, with a quadrant in hand,
attempts to find the altitude of Arcturus,
Magellan accompanying off the coast of Congoland,
but the plumb bob sways- upheaval in sea's palace.
As he squints through the sight, he muses on rank-
his own, the order in his ship,
that of the stars, not in regimental rows or flanks-
they seem diffuse, free, wild in sky skip.
Half-clouds run veiling the sphere's lights;
through his quadrant he sights Phoenix-
quickly clouds cover all; the sky's now graphite.
His work spoilt for him, another indignity impolitic.
"Clean that deck, boy," yells a burly big tar;
adventure can be also rough, dirty, and hard.

XXXVII

A cosmotherium of glass with gold plate,
the bubble restrained by a belt of sea's divisions,
a golden central sun, though the workings, brass, wait,
when the stars' orbits spin, a tune plays, sweet provision.
A child stands by it, one dressed as her mother,
a child-adult, pondering with many sighs
the complexity, the wonder of this curious other,
which turns and sings as the stars' paths arise.
Her father rushes in and scolds his child;
she's not to play with his scientific tools;
neither to be by the telescope or backstaff, beguiled;
she must play only with flowers, with dolls- his rules.
She narrows her eyes and stares at his back;
the cosmotherium in his hands, now running off track.

XXXVIII

A woman sits peering through a telescope,
dressed in white frilly cap and collar over black,
scope seven feet, lenses made with hope;
she's Caroline Herschel, star sighting heaven's track.
A late night stargazer, her brother, complains;
he must have tea and bread toasted and buttered;
she helps him, drawn away, more erratic in domain
than the wildest comet ever wonder ice uttered.
She discovers one "hairy star" more, this night-
(eight in her lifetime, a scholar's feat),
but as she does, an infant wails, world stage fright;
she must tend to her nephew, and the fire sweep.
Late she stays awake, an initiate clear
to the masculine club, of studying revolutions of the
crystalline sphere.

XXXIX

Emily Dickinson's thinking she's living on the continent-
she stares one rainy afternoon at an armillary sphere,
earth and moon encaged by argument.
The day a haze of splendor, she daydreams here.
Arctic circle, ecliptic, horizon ring, tropic of cancer,
celestial equator, meridian ring, equinoctial colure,
sostitial colure, which when whirled like a dancer,
makes one dizzy with the competing paths' lure.
She muses too deeply on possibility,
a small vision of the infinite for an hour
and ponders, "How hard to be first cause, stability,
if it means as well, direction of all, not cowards."
"Happily for the One, the First," she thinks,
"there's untold numbers of angels helping," her hands
stained with ink.

XL

Dressed in a rough white robe, with sandals worn,
a man with smooth hair walks on the rocky, dusty path.
He glows like amber in the high sun of noon;
a few olive trees nod on his behalf.
He pulls out of his pocked a perpetual calendar
from the eighteenth century, looking like a pocket watch,
with days of week, dates of the months, each hour,
astrological symbols, sunrise and sunset, set by pressing a
catch.
He muses on a garden in ancient Persia,
considering the exact year of its construction;
he thinks, the calendar obliges with truth's version,
showing every element of time in the year of its instruction.
Yeshua walks from Asia, where years he's spent;
he has with him the secret of the infinite: eternal present.

XLI

Yeshua, the emblem of perfection,
enters every room to set it astir-
allowing his glow of resurrection,
his hair lit from above, his halo pure.
Unlike the fellows who harbor insurrection,
always his being's revolt is peace's lure.
Yawning with his stretch total frame,
enveloping Emily's lithe self,
she hugs his muscle's long terrain;
he catches her up to heaven: the twelfth.
Unless you can follow, I'll tell the next frame:
apt together, they're married by an elf.
Alpha she calls him, the eternal handsome one;
Alpha he rings his laughter as towards her he runs.

To comprehend time's morality plays,
the experience in Egypt beyond quick scan,
mentioning Pacific islands' three millennium since survey,
pursuing a Persian's and a Hebrew's quotidian.
We'll study these and more: Mauryans,
a Japanese's Empress' excursion and its told tale,
the Byzantine theatrics recorded by historians,
a Tibetan conversion, a nation's alchemy.
These lessons we'll glance at: also, China,
an African horseman's struggle to rule,
a legendary warrior princess, also of Africa,
and warred roses' union in England's Yule.
In Sweden, a lady who left for thought, her crown;
with an Austrian empress, we'll call spun our gown.

XLIII

Experience in Egypt beyond quick scan,
Hatshepsu standing in temple of Deir-el-Bahari
incense and chanting obscuring the columns' plan;
the musty cool inside lingers, belays sunheat worry.
First level barbarian, second level mystery;
on what level did Hatshepsu walk?
The pharaoh ship monumental flowed stormlessly;
if questioned an individual, yet never the crown's rock.
What did she think as she stalked in a mystery temple,
at the back a god half-beast, foreign?
Hatshepsu was born into this fiat simple;
to rule was the sacred part, not the citizen.
Now we see complexity of a different sort;
sacred in all, yet what's unholy, purity doesn't thwart.

XLIV

Mentioning Pacific islands' three millennium since survey,
more democratic in their government
with small settlements of handfuls, there's still play,
their tales not of kings, yet mythologically bent.
It is enough- games, food, drink, and work?
They too knew war, two ways-
for territory or for womenfolk,
else breathing shifting bough's beauty for centuries' days.
Nature bountiful in taro, yam, or fruit,
other proteins discovered in ocean, an intoxicating brew:
some women have lived so for history's entire route;
the daily life's enough for an eternal view,
because the ocean in its thunder and sapphire,
spoke enough mystery and wildness to inspire.

Pursuing a Persian's and a Hebrew's quotidian,
we seek a king and Esther in their palace,
with couches of like swans
resting on the floor's malachite and lapis looking glass.
Robed in the idea ascension,
they speak together at night late in their reign,
of things of the spirit placed in time's invention.
So fairy tales are woven on earth's terrain.
There is the power play behind each scepter's rule,
thousands wounded painfully because of the sway
from deeper than despot or just king- the school
of our life that is to tell evil's from good's array.
What I read in the richness of Esther's surprising song,
is that good is made harsh by the efforts of wrong.

XLVI

We'll study further, more; Mauryans.
I order myself and my words- my domain.
To prevail over self, Gupta, Ashoka, artisans,
knew as the necessary step for a zenith suzerain.
The difficulties of rule are not mine:
the budget portioning, the close administration;
army raising, speaking to a public benign.
I share with them only renunciation;
I'm glad that they discovered a spiritual path.
One turned towards pure spirit, gave up his crown,
the other denied further due, violence, wrath.
One Jain, one Buddhist: saint-kings, both astound.
My only kingdom flows with the ink;
it's also of imagination, the stories that I link.

Of a Japanese empress' excursion and its told tale,
I'll speak: Empress Jingo sailed Korea to conquer,
Sin Ra, and a tempest arose when a whale
bore up the fleet's boats. The miracle they lived to confer-
she was successful, temporarily.
The moral I gather from these pieces reads:
the first to consider in foreign policy
is one's relations with heaven: let it all else precede!
Divinity's intervention (which angel exactly,
I cannot say, sent the great fish,)
speaks volumes: approval of female rule tacitly,
and approval of faith in the miraculous.
Because each breath derives from an angel's thought,
we must look for the uncommon by uncommon sought.

XLVIII

The Byzantine theatrics recorded by historians,
Justinian ruling, Theodora tending to beauty;
he changed the law to marry that Grecian-
for senators and actresses, separation was a duty.
Perhaps he believed the studied lines,
the regal gestures and carriage, accustomed to costume,
of Theodora, and the romantic wildness of intertwine,
would help him win the Byzantium throne room.
It did: decadence, or social innovation?
How can prejudice be hurled against
the fate of all, as each earth citizen
is called upon to act in dress foreign, impermanent?
Except for we two: we have been our selves-
what we are, the deepest truth tells!

XLIX

A Tibetan conversion, a nation's alchemy:
Srong-lotsan-sgampo and his wife
favored Buddhism for their country's chemistry
to mix into a spiritual kingdom, a pageantry-full life.
Was it a sensitive king and a queen attuned
to possibility for diversity development,
or was it fate's cogs turning inevitably, knorten-runed,
towards heaven's telesis envelopment?
Splendor is born of imagination and of work,
and the originality and uniqueness of Tibet-
llama's silk robes, the Potala's painted gold eaves,
all offerings from each Tibetan person's goblet.
These genealogies do not conflict;
king, peasant, angel, all history benedict.

L

An African horseman's struggle to rule
I speak now of: that makes me griot.
Sundiata Keita, another lion king with choirs
of African bards who about fires sing, of overthrow.
First unable to walk, it saved his life-
Sumanguru wouldn't kill the boy.
A turn: he learned to stand, walk, ride,
then Keita warred five years his victory to enjoy.
The inclusion of this tall African,
noble in deep eyes proud stance and voice bold,
leaves out his current status; time's span
does not always end with death's toll.
Does he dream of Africa of dust spun,
or know of empires there underneath strong sun?

LI

A legendary warrior princess, also of Africa,
blessed with confidence wildness and with strength,
made of Zazzu an empire with that formula.
She conquered Katsana, Kano, a list of towns at length.
Sarauriya Amina walked the mythic line
between the known, historically probable,
and the tales told by firelight, by starshine,
vague historical memories, fable.
I believe she rode in Zazzauland,
a cloth wrapped around to keep dust out,
defying detractors or the shimmering sand-
the force that opposes women, she did rout.
I write to show my faith in women's warrior being,
as well to hope that to many her story I bring.

LII

The warred roses' union in England's Yule:
in January Fourteen-Eighty-Six,
Henry Tudor married Elizabeth of York, by rule
of the people, tranquility to preserve, hurts to fix.
He wasn't ruled inwardly by that decree;
his wife he treated with some harshness,
angered no doubt by his inability
to choose his own mate, though she was sweetness.
How could love succeed, when force was its administration?
The force of pressure to marry, of his displeasure,
their irascibility, that each couldn't choose their
ministration?
The command to love thus out of measure.
They followed the script much too closely; were men
to tend sheep and women to rule, there would be peace
then!

LIII

In Sweden, Christina left for thought, her crown.
Placed on the throne at age sixteen,
because of her father's battlefield death, her renown
she abdicated at twenty-two, hating routine.
Rather than, regent, conscript for clash,
or ministers consult with to minimize conflict,
she loved so philosophy, thoughts' fountain splash,
fine arts, antiquities, criticism intermixt,
that the world's busyness, correction and control
of people and events, she denied due,
for correction and control of her own mind and soul,
her evolving self of intellect's and not politic's hue.
Consumed later by what she'd given away,
she must remember that power is story, self, and play.

With an Austrian Empress' story, spun is our gown.
Maria Theresa inherited a throne.
Queen of Hungary, Bohemia, of many towns,
part Netherlands, Milan, Mantua, an empire long sown.
Frederick of Prussia felt hungry for more land,
so the new queen needed to raise armies to fight.
Walking to the hall where the populace stands,
(tall ceilings, all marble), her apprehension in sight.
She swept into the room, small yet brave,
and before the people asked for an army raised.
Their answer thundered through the enclave;
it's spell, love, devotion, stayed with her for days.
"Pro reginae vitam et sanguinem consecramus."
Evidence of heaven's glory on earth with us.

History Lessons to Instruct Morally
LV

King Mu in Korea dreamed a messianic kingdom,
but most kingdoms are built by blood shedding battle.
Not so thine, red dragon, noble, pure, crowned;
thou not like pirates, but more gently renowned.
Thy rule over earth only granted by agree, tenanted
thy kingdoms sun-clad, cloud-fed, nun-led.
Any sweet kingdom here soon routed by might's play,
though wandering on plains of paradise is a shepherd's day.
That conquest best, that is friendship's, of enmity, of death.
Self-conquest best made before last breath.
Mine is simple compared with all these, more mild;
my simpleness is play like a child's.
We find in being the entrance to heaven on earth-
many the mysteries of spirit, seen here through rebirth.

King Mu in Korea dreamed a Messianic kingdom
after by a lake a vision past him swam.
He built on hundreds of acres, a temple complex
to house three emanations of Miruk, the pretext.
His son fond of the savage power game war,
neglected the stone structures for the avatar,
so the temples rapt with jungle vines decayed.
The largest complex ever complexified with new array.
I won't moralize with my first thought,
that earthly splendor's eternity can't be bought;
rather, I'll ponder and the meaning debate;
would ever a true Messiah would himself sultanate?
One generation glory, the spiritual intent right;
is it that society's program here is against truth and light?

Most kingdoms built by bloodshedding battle;
more blood spilt for more territory, more chattel,
but this men's game soldiers still adore.
Territory also language, art, literature gained by war.
Lifting a silver chalice of mead in a muddy hand,
kings of Scotland's tenth century land,
extended their rule some small land to win.
They wanted his lordship acknowledged by Celtic kin.
Of Northumbria, called tyrant, great king,
has firm told for their strengths bold offspring.
Yet why do males love so, intransigence?
Do one half of men crave war's pence?
Is this planet a gathering place
for the violent, or is it progress' slow pace?

LVIII

Arthur, red dragon, noble, pure, crowned-
whale won strength, knowing sea song treasures, renowned;
I see thee and Arthur as one magelord.
Both wizard and king, thou rulest by love, by word.
The apprentice tale not of me or of thee:
thou pure might from birth, thyself body from sea,
true puissance that in attack stays calm,
perfection in all points, thou my fears' balm.
I speak of thee, not of other kings,
but Thou in my dreams, art Lord of the Ring,
of the earth and space, walk King- also a troubadour,
of spinning planets' knowledge an author.
Depths of the oceans some given to know;
thy depths my study, myself my only trousseau.

Thou not like Arab princes, whom pirates insult,
in being more wild than many worthy salts,
throwing themselves into excess of energy!
Packing into their selves all this synergy:
raiding on fine horses, camel caravans,
fighting battles in desert against barbarians,
enjoying a multitude of fair women's embrace;
ascending many levels to Ka'bah, Merkbah, apace.
Lives with riotous adventure-
we more genteel- they buccaneer brash, no censure!
I wish we too could throng with world action
our lives, our selves garb with a faithful faction.
Truth: I'd rather study and see you in sleep found
than see our ideas read by wicked thoughts' sound.

LX

Rule of Novgorod only granted
by the Kiptchack Khanate, so highbred
Novgorod princes many times
to the Golden Horde Throne climbed.
Tartar sovereignty absolute, the Mongols
deep in furs over layers of silk drank from bowls
while incense clouds burning in braziers
obscured the carpeted floors, walls, for seers.
The tableau is distant: distant the power too
from will or consent of ruled. True,
if everyone could rule themselves, the would be no need
for government. That's heaven indeed.
Here the unscrupulous pretend with blood stained swords
to work for money, fame. What's the truth, interred?

Some kingdoms are sun-clad, cloud-fed, monk-led.
Ogodon Khan from his pleasure dome fled
to Tibet, to conquer a pearl for his chest.
He gave its rule to a llama of the Sakya sect.
Did he wait long enough from mist to sun,
to view the dance of the monks hard won,
the dance of strength to drive demons at bay,
not importunate prayer, conviction folded away?
Tibet's self-reliance- in food, in wool,
in religion, all by themselves tooled,
their own built paradise, he must have noted
to give themselves to themselves, not to others instead.
I'd give them their own if it were mine:
I give thee thyself, thou aren't someone else's sign.

LXII

One sweet kingdom routed by might's play,
as the Anhuac, elegant bards of delicacy's way,
of mild polished manners and skilled in all arts,
with Nezahualcoyotl ruling all a confederacy's parts,
were overcome by their fierce neighbors bedecked,
once allied with the genteel Anhuac, in check;
their human sacrifice belief's thirst for victims
in the capital's war temple, caught up flesh in addiction.
So the crueler over the less cruel gained temporary
reknown,
still, we tell of a secret read from power's rune:
on earth, when some part is sacrificed
to strength, including love, intellect, then the vice
of brute might grows like the iron man,
who is all muscle and no grace or thought of span.

LXIII

Wandering on plains of paradise is a shepherd's kingdom,
the keen air crisp with meadow flower scents and hum,
the orchard and gardens below suspended in air,
the llama keepers walking in clouds and soft sun flare.
In Peru's early hours of autonomy of villages,
the peace of the people of mountain lineage
contrasted extension by wise and temperate policy
with later empire craving, fighting more ferociously.
Tupac Yupanqui in Atacama's deserts;
noise, dust, dirt, blood, pain, sobs by sword convert
in the valleys, the dust of the hills.
A kingdom gained, and for what, save thrill?
The shepherd at the river as the army thundered past,
his solitude and nature's smoke trampled in the grass.

That conquest best, that is friendship's of enmity,
so also Tupac Yupanqui demonstrated with amity.
I'll speak of him further, of his connections
with Ecuador, the Carayan kingdom's subjection.
The Andean earned the title Huainacapac,
the Great or the Conqueror, after he attacked
Quito's empire. He showed in arts of peace
an adept also, with his romantic ease.
He married a daughter of the Carayan tribe,
the conquered. Never again to Cuzco he would ride;
rather, he governed thirty-eight prosperous years,
for a temporary union which didn't persevere.
His sons divided his kingdom in two,
then the Spaniards arrived for deathly rendezvous.

Self conquest best made before a person's death,
so we think of the scenes of last breath.
if Lorenzo de Medici wanted to repent, to confess;
and then three questions of him by Savanorola were
pressed.
Do you think you are good? No, slow.
Can you refrain from sin? No.
Will you become pure and leave others free?
The answer no, so no absolution, conviction's fee.
Could the wish of a sinner to attain
a high station disguise the truth of a saint?
What as the sway of sinners who oppose?
The question left is, after death, where do saints and sinners
repose?
Could Lorenzo to heaven be sent not to hell to mend?
Who can say to what salvation after death we wend?

LXVI

Mine is simple, compared with all these kingdoms:
the shifting nuances of capability, that sing some,
such as Henry II, Diane of Potiers
and Catherine de Medici's dance cavalier.
The triune power play of passions,
both erotic and irascible, like the sun's fashion
of moving between tree's branches in patterns
the depths and light combined as sense's attars.
These once angels' workings were morality's undoings,
so the only morality left was, of choosing
between power and love, and love the substratum
that informed this ruling pageant: love ultimatum.
I rescind that context: there are many
who of love's complexities choose not to love any.

My simpleness is play like a child's,
to live within the kingdom of bliss, wild,
the invisible perfect world, of living in the spirit
which wraps one up in transcendence to inspirit.
I know of one who lived this life, amongst buffalo.
Pretty Shield, a medicine woman of the Crows.
She transmitted the legacy of her perfect life,
far more perfectly than any of these rulers' strife.
She knew play, imagination, acceptance in faith
of empirically unverifiable, knew of wraiths,
mermaids, fairies, and remained pure
though death and cruelty felled some around her.
An epic life of higher being. Vignette: riding scared
amongst the thundering buffalo herd.

LXVIII
Thou My Lord

We find in being the entrance to heaven on earth,
placing ourselves in dialogue with all of worth,
extending ourselves through the knowledge of
other climates, cultures, kings, queens, love.
The accumulation of being throughout the ages,
forms a question of itself for all sages;
how much must we know, can we know, and what?
What precedence shall we give to what thought?
The deeper we search, and know, the deeper still, we.
I see in myself, lost in this tumultuous sea,
so small, yet not meaningless, of such a value;
that my being's found worth in Thee, is true.
I find my meaning in our wedded union;
my love for Thee and Thine for me, Thou, being's lion.
My being's Thy scion.

The Lost World
LXIX

The world of comprehension gathers to us
as the world begins to fall apart.
We've delved these treasures of the earth's repoire,
while billions of stories dry to dust, towards infinity.
Each thought and perception bundle, each human,
working weary not towards glory but for grace,
fling more into their treasure of experience,
while they plow and chop the earth to abandon.
Thus as wisdom, knowledge, and complexity ascend,
as delicacy of thought and spirit sometimes glow,
the earth and its beings- the ant people,
the tree people, the wolf and wild people, languish.
Our other shaped fellows, Gaia, the waters, wilt.
It's as though in their storytelling humans the earth part
unbuilt.

LXX

Fell and build, fell and build, thoughtlessly,
birthing billions to fit many kingdoms into one;
thus the Gaia mantle, paper thin, is reft
of its anterior garden self-definition.
The ignorance and violence of all of us
replaces desert for forest, dust for green,
and thus the world of law crushes underneath
the passion of luxuriant dense canopies.
So is returned, for abundance beauty and life,
wastes, ripped the mantle of green from the earth.
Gaia, turning molten mass core, earth rock thick,
water, and light shifting continental plates,
throws tempests of anger, whirlwind, volcano, flood,
storm, earthquake. Appease? Only accepting a new garden.

LXXI
Each Tree Spirit on Death is Released to a
Pristine Eternal Forest

Should we pray this is not now a dying planet,
spinning slowly towards complete destruction,
should we pray the human evil does not choke itself
into oblivion and all sentient creatures with it,
and should we pray that the bounty of care, the tree
hugging,
the replanting, the thrift and ecosystem concern,
pray these do cumulate in the earth's
resurrection in a garden state:
still one must choose for one's self, the upper path,
the love and nonviolence for every bird animal fish being,
for each tree within one's circumference,
must choose the peace that pulls the pure of heart
to Heaven when their true self floats
free of the dusty machine confines and the new life began.

LXXII

We won't speak of heaven's sufferless perfection
which we shall find in light body's resurrection.
All that I find of it, it's relics here,
are found only in a heart clear.
For a beauty's steps tread on ants,
a glass vase's grace takes swelter dissonant,
the price of gold is a miner's hack,
our homes repress and gash the earth's back.
Think: the wild bee's flights madurya sweet,
the birds tremor trill in rain or in heat,
the cats that love with their whole body's waking,
the horses that men forgive the quaking.
I see man's insistence on himself as first, the first sin;
he wrecks for pride, heavenly nature's rhythm.

LXXIII

My cats sometimes kill a bird, a being miniature,
as we speak: poor perfect of stature!
That my sweet companions should covet to kill
is unspeakable horror- yet they know not but thrill.
Little birds! Soon to heaven spend!
Thou wilt live forever, I vow my beloveds,
in a perfect paradise peredezia, mostly not hunted
any more by cats; what peace, by tongue unsaid!
My cats and ye little birds shall be friends!
Some wilt sit on their shoulders, past amended!
For thy perfection of spirit, thou art unsurpassed.
Innocent beings, I salute ye as elegiast!
Oh, I hate the foul ideas and their cruelty intertwined
into every heart and into every mind!

LXXXIV

In this twice weighted universe where we seek not union,
everything's a shadow and a corruption of itself.
The heavenly cat robs not anything of its motion wealth,
the birds there sing unburdened by babies, are pure paean.
Our bliss here, which not often we can find,
our lives being more painful than pastoral,
our bliss will be naught to that ideal
of joy and passion which waits before us in mind.
I fear Thee though, and the life of the elite,
the angels before us each exquisite in being
so mighty, wise, quick, exotic on seeing
that my heart will falter as I gaze at that fleet.
I'm afraid of the glory that stuns all;
I'm afraid of Thy brilliance, me being so small.

Passion Plays
LXXV
Is Love Only to Endure Torment?

But I spoke of rulers, not of lovers.
Rulers aren't lovers: they've no privacy for play.
Let me ponder if I can say with sweetness
something of lovers while they're in the earth.
Who are the lovers then that sit musing in the shade?
This earth is separation for lovers;
there's instead, temporary unions that bring sadness more.
Then what type of love is here on earth found?
I can't find much depth of passion in eyes,
nor can I discover fineness of nobility in spirit.
What I discover instead is a corrupting band,
an earth that seeks to reft lovers apart.
They try the loving intentions to kill, with their vice:
vulgarity, cruelty, thoughtlessness, a heart of ice.

LXXVI
I Find no Passion in Their Eyes

Lovers' spent passion is the earth's torture;
they spend their passion on others than their loves
and those with the deepest passion
are sickened by coarseness enough to monkish censure.
Passion isn't capable to withstand
the angriness of the rabble,
so passion waits unexpressed save for moments
when it starts, surprised, our for a second's flash.
Thus the earth's lovers play a cold game;
they turn themselves within their prison bodies,
to stare into the eyes of a temporary lover,
knowing it's for love that they play that way.
For love, and yet for hate: those opposites
polarize the lovers more, whose passion in hell or heaven
was kept.

LXXVII
Sinners and Saints

For lovers sift, upon the earth, heaven and hell,
and they sift and mix between their siftings bitter
knowledge of hierarchies, of truces, of war,
of the mighty bending down to taste the small.
Or so the mighty say. For they're worn
by the water torture cruelty of everyday,
the corrupting language which angels abhor,
the insulting dredging which on the good pours.
So the intermingling of savage and of sweet,
means the loser is love, for love's further treat.
Love is overwon so that it all can capture;
love undone and crying is love's further rapture.
For the prize won by those few who renounce,
is this: heaven's beauty and bliss unmarred, I announce.

LXXVIII
The Body Can Be a Prison

Love between the shadow plays of life,
the self fashioned into another flowing self;
our true being of splendor, superior to decay,
hides locked within our flesh bodies.
The body holds the spirit within it,
to a magickless timeful predestined round,
the machine of our selves set in specifics:
we can't overcome the limitations unsound.
What does that mean for love, for love play?
It's an act and a show and involves not depths.
Our deepest selves buried within our selves,
so what's given out is only deep as genetic's shallow day.
I feel trapped within myself; I'm hiding below;
I rose to radiance once, where love himself clear would
grow.

Love tumultuous, love like a sea's pull,
the grandeur of dizziness, the fervent way,
the exuberance of a child's wildness,
love private and particular, the endless day-
these for me aren't, not now, for my low self-
I want them in my future to flower overspilt,
in heaven's gold lights on unspoiled meadows,
Thy complete being my passionate stay.
I see Thee as Thou art now, as a shield-
stun my senses, in chariots wheeled-
Thou the gentle actor of a blameless part,
Thy tender thunder now kept close in my heart.
Michael- with little of my past until ascend-
I feel trapped in my mind until higher I wend.

LXXX

I ferret, in love, the ontological difference
betwixt sinners and saints, lovers and liars.
This passion will I tell, more than only
the seven deadly sins, is corrupting poison:
Hate, the hate that forms all sins,
anger lust greed envy cruelty-
the hate that most often suits itself in love,
or in normality, so it can ordinary play.
Love is the complexity, the most beautiful work;
hate simplifies and brutalizes the sinner.
Love is a degree that is endless to learn;
hate is the monotone dull, absurd.
Love then, the sinners! That's the greatest challenge:
it's like loving the pit, or a creature-filled dark cave.

LXXXI

I ken a world with foundation of aggression,
the root boast of work, of lust, of false beauty,
of building, of higher nature's suppression.
The city sparrow knows as it flies sooty
in a quick fling from a car or a cat, fleet,
that what humans have made, is intolerant
of the timid, the rare, the gentle, the sweet.
The world cherishes anvils, axes, guns as it's sacrosanct.
Where are the gentle women, the gentle men?
Instead there is flared temper to exhaustion,
scenes of lawlessness, evilness untold, when
all gentility and charity now is viewed with precaution.
I long for my habitat true, a heaven of citizens
who sow not these tares, being's corruptions.

LXXXII
Where Do the Extinct Go?

When I grow about my house inventive green,
emerging patterns of emerald energy emitting,
I change the status quo of old shrubs' songs,
and replace with new fences, hedges, borders long,
the patterns there, imprinting my creativity,
and thus I impose upon the earth's natural proclivity.
This section small of land that I plant,
when multiplied by the people extant,
becomes a monstrous reworking of
the earth's energy- it isn't love!
Nature's own selection of youngness limited,
and this suppresses the other magic citizens,
those for whom the world once was home,
those who flying lit with hope towards heaven must roam.

LXXXIII
Love the Bewilderer

My thought when on homo sapiens I think,
is of the selfishness that pushes to the brink,
the waterfall waters of Gaia's life-
the selfishness that claims for death, green's fife.
Oh men and women with terrible teeth!
Worse than an ocelot or a jaguar- you wreath
the earth with fire, with smoke, with heat!
In your uncontrolled ruttings, fleet
comes the world's destruction, after
your evolution emerged your killing pattern.
That the highest is the lowest, I declare!
Man is the beast, not the lynx or the bear!
I'm ashamed that so many were birthed
to try to kill the world and the birds' mirth.

LXXXIV
Further Misanthropy

Let me tell of that which we must overcome of hate;
to hate the buildings built of stones ripped
from the mountains' bones;
to hate the machines spewing gas that condenses
to nibble at the high northern forests;
to hate the complexes built on the territory
of finches, warblers, orioles, wrens;
to wonder at the women through the ages
who birthed without thought, overmuch;
to wonder at the men who killed the forests,
who forced others to sweat underground,
who damned the rivers, who tortured and ate the cattle;
Ask why! Ask why! For this world is of perishable orchid,
and of nearly imperishable human hands.

LXXXV

Enough of pain's preponderance.
Seeking past the obvious hindrance,
I will try to capture something of love's goodness
though to tell it taxes the mind with madness.
In the bird's pairs, the sweetness there
of lilting arduous labor together
is the best love bounty that I can find,
far better than the cantankerous games of mind.
Let us learn ourselves to gentle, refine,
until as the delicacy of the bird we sip wine
of devoted care, of harmlessness, of beauty,
with ahimsa becoming our childlike duty.
My wont leans to talk of birds and not men,
for it is the doves and not humans who are my kin.

LXXXVI

How can we in the world escape to safety,
to privacy, to peace, to love, to beauty?
Will it be a flight of the mind,
that will proffer us our paradise find?
Or will it be fancy, or thickets verdant,
or a celestial soar of starry extent?
I bind fast, first, about my home,
this hedge: myrtle, laurel, planted in the loam,
germander's gentle knot, borders of boxwood.
Then about my mind I enclose as I should
myself with mazes of endeavor's will-
I save myself, my self, thus to give Thee Thy fill.
In the earth there is no shelter perfect spun
save one: towards Thy mind's garden I run.

The love that I seek daily with my love,
oh Michael! seems heavens away from me,
as if the imposition of the imperfect's harsh fee,
the body that is an act and that far from bliss roves,
bewilders my simple mind with obstacles' troves;
I seek Thee and find Thee not: what Thou art
I know not, except Thy difficult part,
which is Thy distance from Thy dove.
For Thou not a word against pain, start,
nor betray Thy incognito self,
with more than a touch or a word; my health,
of spirit, thus bottled, swoons, thus hushed my heart.
I cannot search for that which is withheld
Thyself, Thy spirit, a shadowy distant spell.

LXXXVIII

Thyself, thy spirit, casting a shadowy distant spell,
let us plant more than a garden of dappled hue;
let us together, though Thou hide thyself anew,
play a larger part than we'd first tell.
Thus not only trees to plant, but a view,
of the potential sharing of forests pristine,
forever to keep them unspoilt, Edenic clean,
or a view of the self when freed from wickedness' stew.
Planting in more than dust; in spirits, even mean,
the energy and effort to achieve what's high,
or the angelic capability of purity like the sky,
which is a unity untouched and not parceled by machine.
Is this Thy love? Or is Thine for me,
Thy most important work, and understanding's key?

LXXXIX

What Thy most important work, Thy understanding's key;
what Thy work's extent, Thy energy's boundaries?
Where does myth and man meet and where part vagary?
How do I know what is of Thee and what of me?
For I revise thy boundaries daily; what's customary
is to find a new empire entire of Thy being,
of knowledge, of sacrifice, of tenderness of foreseeing,
Thy nobility of the hidden hard won kingdom legendary.
Art Thou Thy most important work, guaranteeing
what can be created by Thee- around Thee else
nothing; and then, who Thee formed, what indwells
in Thee of divinity, with the infinite agreeing?
Thou spoke to me this answer once, of God's quest,
that the infinite is always seeking itself, love being the best.

XC

The infinite always seeks itself, love being the best.
What is God is both simple and complex;
the simple part of love and helpfulness, no check,
the complex, what is, the forms, the structures, life's
bequest.
And thus I know of Thee through time's daily trek,
more than I would know just with Thee to speak;
I know the eternal husbandman in Thee to seek,
and the cosmic warrior who travels parsec.
Parsec for my being, being close to Thy peak,
I grow thus warmed by Thy sun's rays,
by Thy satellite's pull- our friends be praised!
by both, I grow to more than my former speck.
For, before I knew Thee, I had only passion-
now with Thee I have logic, comprehension, compassion.

XCI

Now Thou hast logic, comprehension, compassion,
and what Thou art is what Thou art,
for though Thy completion is hidden in part,
still Thou, kind, loving, gentle, sweet, my salvation.
For what I owe to Thee of my mind apart
from the tedious small confinement of my start, not an end,
from the internal warring on which enemies depend,
is that of myself I owe Thee all my art.
Thy gifts to me of riches extend,
yet Thou keep Thyself free from money's taint-
Thy greatest gifts me with Thy constant wonder acquaint;
but were Thou poor I'd still my love extend.
For Thy best largesse is Thy own self;
I harbor Thee to keep Thee to myself.

XCII

I harbor Thee to keep Thee to myself,
or at least so I try Thee to keep,
with Thy help, for Thou hast wisdom's sweep,
to give a stylized fiction to the world of Thyself.
This I'll tell, of public and private leap;
between them there is a difference;
the myth is purposefully removed, with different
circumference,
and the man, not static but flowing deep.
So the famous, simplified after life intense,
drop the persona of limitations and clichés;
all move from corruption's to incorruption's way,
but the public pays tribute to ashes, to their interpretation's
pretense.
I know the body as a hindrance to perfection;
I know the material keeps some from seeing the
resurrection.

I know the material keeps some from seeing the
resurrection,
or to the miracle of each daisy's growth,
though Thou me taught of the awe of each life oath;
from the buttercup to the cypress, immoderation.
Thy life and Thyself for me are amazement's troth;
I wonder at each existence's magic,
of which the self-willed fact and present form quick
shocks me with the central motion, that One created both.
Which One is that which created consciousness' work?
He hides so perfectly from His creation,
the denizens of which are aware of themselves for
avocation,
but which can't detect and worship their Creator maverick.
I think Thou knowest which One is that Dove,
the Love that I seek with my love.

Passion Stays
XCIV
Is It Love?

Of passion, I could write that it's absence is dormancy,
that it spins in all birds' wings and throats,
that it pulls the bee to the rose's luxuriancy,
that it thinks not small a fire compared to stars afloat,
that it pushes the streams' songs' opulency,
that it stirs in the wind as it passes remote,
that it drives the buds to open in fluency,
that it pushes the heart to feel the complete note.
I lie! None of these are passion's claim-
they're generous, evolved, contained, spiritual-
what they are is perhaps love, or being, their frame.
Passion is rarer than rubies or perfect pearls
and perhaps takes a journey below to reclaim,
the truth of it sometimes a difficult pursual.

XCV
The Deeper Truth

I could think of passion passionlessly
of what there was in my youth too innocent
the passion that pulled me fearlessly
into the days to live mellifluent,
as if soaring in air my mind noiselessly-
this passion was hidden bewilderment.
For I did not know then of passion's fact:
there is none in the world- that dimension
is like the fourth and too hard to attract
in the dense body of imperfection pollution.
It is all feigned, all a sham
save one kind which to apprehension
hides; the angels' source ideogram
for their selfless sacrifice: their lives' invention.

Many obstacles there are to Thee, love,
Thyself art one, and time is one more
and agency's difficult work to journey above,
which all set up pillars behind and before,
to pace my journey to our mind's meeting,
Thou being my sight and my chore
to turn myself into an eternal tender greeting,
so Thou know that joy is still in store.
Oh, soul of mind and spirit fine spun!
What battles I face to be made
like my love who has already perfection won!
Sweet passion, I pray for thee, be not afraid!
Carry me towards that alterless altar, the Aeternal One
of my future passion's goal, in passion arrayed!

XCVII

I recall once when Thy higher self
overtook Thy habitual self and Thou awoke
with the vigor of highest youth and with the activity of mind
spoke to me wild and exotic,
so my friend turned into stranger anew.
What Thou said then I cannot recall;
I only remembered that Thou had energy
that turned all Thy flesh to quick synergy.
Give me this truth- will I Thee find
in the midst of the others whose bodies not Thine
wander to wonder in the halls above?
Will I find Thee quickly within a word, love?
I will seek Thee wherever thou go,
for I understand only how we are tied past woe.

The Mystical Marriage
XCVIII

I will tell now of the secrets that I hold,
those that I received from thy instruction,
what I learned by listening to silence,
what I know from seeing the invisible,
what by learning the unlearnable I have been told,
what reading the unwritten was my introduction,
that which for sensing the psychic I have paid more than
pence,
that by living the alchemical marriage I know as a sibyl.
The secrets will explain the reason here for evil,
and history's wild creative intercessions
with myth and magic and perfection's prevention.
A handful of knowledge only will I scatter;
then discover some mystery sessions
that will plant not hope but comprehension.

What this society will receive for choosing
evil for its gods and not the true Divinity
is the whirlwind born of sowing wind;
do not choose the energy of chaos and destruction.
do not choose the wasting,
the burnt axed rainforest lungs' torn synergy,
mass starvations, terrible war, (which they defend-)
their choice of sow fire and reap the fire construction.
This phenomenal civilization has over time
slowly tried to destroy Nature, evil's largess,
killing recklessly as much as they could,
these the faithless and perverse generation
of whom Jesus spoke. What is their punishment?
For choosing evil will its own punishment find.

C

What it means to be reborn is solely
the cycle of rebirth of those confined here,
but also a clean ego repentance:
no more pitting one's self and one's will
against goodness, kindness, wholly
or secretly, subtly as many do with cheer,
with every cruel act, concupiscence,
murder, warring, perversion zeal.
Rather study these virtues to exhibit;
become sweet, innocent, happy, obedient,
thoughtful of other's joys, delicate,
with no hidden agenda intellectual to inhibit.
I tell thus how to be reborn lucent,
though they know already love's dictates.

CI

Cultural formation the kingdom of heaven on earth,
costumes dishes dances music love plays
all forming a stage for the mystical marriage,
marriage the perfection of bliss's potentiality.
Thus the players of both sky and land birth,
act in intrigues and loves of war's days,
the planet being continually filled by pilgrimage,
the secrets of the wedding the central key.
We two together know peace, calm,
understanding, stability of faithfulness,
charity, nobility, truth, eternal love,
help each other develop and grow; are balm,
turn to each other and outwards too, bless
though Thou my tutor I call: Me Thou wove.

Our kingdom is not less than this, I tell:
what is high, holy, of heaven here lent
the hidden kingdom of glory within hell,
sacrifice by sweet strong spirits spent
their efforts like a lark's withstanding storm,
to sing to hush the wind and water's form.
Each human hides within their single mind
a higher purpose and possibility
which work is colored and is cloaked I find
in rich hues of love, love the key
to comprehension of how the mighty dwell
with the wicked who here cast dark spell.
Our kingdom resides within the minds and hearts;
the distant heavens form the other parts.

Part Two

The Courtly Romances of Sapphire Pleiades

Introduction

These several dozen sonnets are by no means all of the sonnets that I have enscribed; they are merely some of the odd series that I have been inspired to within a decades long association with that small and beauteous gems quality form, the sonnet. Whenever I feel to create one of these handicraft, instantly the words tumble out like opals from a velvet cloth of the mind and then they shine upon the page with depths of emerald cut facets; so natural and yet so disciplined.

Their subject matter meanders like a country road in a painting by Constable, and yet they are all of the subject matter of Life, the setting of which- the seasons- are displayed- the musicians of which- the birds- are tuning up their viols- the companions of which- the cats- are reprimanded and then praised- next the ladies of the court appear- from all over the world- the God of which next appears and must be wrestled with for his stern tramping upon the court- so he turns himself into a courtier- and the pleadings for help from his barrage shift into a courtier's wisdom yet written at last! from the female perspective- then to culminate the future is pondered- beyond the last passing away of earth- the cessation of passion- the self beyond time contemplated...

These words from one who has dropped out, tuned in, and turned on finally to the noblesse oblige of leisure and the life of the mind; may there always be the view from space for me is my wish and then you the reader can shift towards the hyperspace of the genteel, for good taste and good poetry are never out of fashion never out of place and there can be found room for it even in the Terra of tough tones and incessant tribal beat.

I pray these little and deep lights will find an audience, that they may be heeded as something worthy to read. *Sapphire Pleiades*

The Four Seasons Quartet
CIII
Autumn: Activation

Under the wild burden of seasoned demise,
the leaves drift to their end with cavalry wonder.
The brave are turned from stalwart to plunder,
and raked from the dust, an autumn sacrifice.
The leaves wind to a turn, enticed,
by the moment of transference, which calls to them clear.
In this gentle battle, its anger less to fear,
they enter the space of brilliance as a vice.
Gracious in martyrdom, the leaf soldiers fall,
hosts to desiccation, the final trial,
as oaks' fastest flurry becomes literal.
Each frond and all autumn, before sorrow's call,
exhales its fervor beautiful beguiled
like a tournament of dancers apocryphal.

CIV
Winter: Whirl

The winter is tense and quiet, a mouthful of cold.
Underneath, deep intent threads upward.
All at once, sentiment is suddenly inspired.
One can learn with ice as well as shallows.
The war of winter is an isolation shocking, a hard word;
the steam of battle and of clouds interpools.
All kites have to the south been cajoled;
ice for weeks lies unmarred.
Such an elegant cold, by flurries so carefully wrought,
advances against the elemental chaos;
stamped in the snow, tracings of beauty and thought.
After the war, the tempests of spring and the moss
of nature will cleanse the worries begot
by the wildness of winter which extols loss.

CV
Spring: Fervor

Winter and spring grapple each other's throats;
the ice waits tense before the spring's glare.
Snow begins to wither and water, to float.
From the jaws of winter, spring snatches its share.
Beating a close sky with a cloak,
the buds within the soil begin to wear
towards the sun with their lightning rote.
A growing fervor pushes them there.
They're as a conscience, which was long stunned,
furrows its way towards the justice that
waits above it like another sun.
The clouds pause, hanging like a pitch
about to turn, then sung in a run.
The moments seam the final, warming stitch.

CVI
Summer: Strength

Rivers like leopards begin to run together,
throwing themselves over the silent straits
of rocks with the passion of cavaliers.
In the violent fray they create
tattle. Ready, the silent glow of state,
robed in shatters of glass, a frank sphere,
rushes into the battle to accelerate
its glow, as the trumpets of breath sear.
Torrents of heat and dust scatter in the sky,
as the memory of winter begins to wither
and the pure fingers of rays warm sighs.
Ghosts of storms past, brandishers
of thunders and of lightnings, monopolize
the space of sky, hot malingerers.

A Crown for the Birds
CVII
Charity for Song Sparrows

Together we hold wild family,
that of birds that live near us shyly.
As we throw them seeds on the earth,
we pursue our interest in their mirth.
The song sparrow, tawny hazel striped,
their tiny bodies hopping and pecking, ripe.
Each two in the spring flower to full flock,
so that we are taking care of a dozen stock.
If we stop from our food giving,
these will wither and might join the elsewhere living.
This teaches all that of charity,
it must be incessant to keep being's titularity.
For their title is that they will be free,
free of breeding of hunger of constant stress, as we.

CVIII
A Day Is Also Song

Free of breeding, of hunger, of constant stress as we,
thus I wish for the robins, with avidity,
why only after they transition to paradise;
why, they must not suffer hell's corruption and vice!
The looking about to find dinner's sum,
the storm that tosses a freshness' strum,
the rest from dusk towards the dawn,
the sunrise greeted with beautiful song.
Each robin's life, as with all urban birds',
is a continual parade of wonder; words
cannot describe the activity of each moment-
for the robin, the dawn is hunger's appeasement.
I pray for thee, robin, that I feed grapes;
I pray thee find the heaven that waits.

CIX
Chickadees at Work

I pray thee find the heaven that waits,
my chickadee of less children by fate,
for I cannot think of any other route
to save thee from the hell made by human brutes.
Thy life hard in a pebble body, cunning with jet things
for a muff and a cap, with ebony edged wings,
snapping up spiders, snails, seeds,
nesting in a feathered mossy bed in need.
Thou catch snails and I scatter for thee grain,
I worry when it's thunder and cry when it rains,
but I can't make thee gryfalcon stout,
with talons or beak or fighting humans clout.
Oh chickadee; thou art so small,
so gentle, yet of living so capable.

CX
Mourning Dove: Evolution's Legacy

Of living thou too art capable, mourning dove,
though delicate and dulcet, though full of love,
which a feat is, to survive evolution's thrusts,
building every year for aeons, your nests.
What hearty heart in thee can brave storms?
Where the source of thy strength, the cuneiform
thou write of being's mystery,
that thy small gray form braved time's fury.
Can it be found in the sweet sad cry
that each cares for their mate and their earth trial,
to birth each year with no choice and no will
that's the kept secret of this planet painful;
that thought and self will are extremely suppressed,
whether in evolution's lowest or in it's highest.

CXI
The House Finch's Song

Whether on the lowest note or in the highest,
thou call house finch with a delightful unrest,
unrest in the joy that is, more burgeons forth
from thy throat, a honey flow golden in worth,
as if to pull to thee and to extend out again
from thy rose and chestnut self, bliss's yen,
so thou, handful, charge currents out
of the usurpation of hope over pain to rout.
Thus beautiful thy few notes' refrain;
if this were heaven, with thy small brain
thou could call any note in any pattern,
and all birds could sing a nightingales' turn.
Thus I'd gift thee, charming dawn blush,
thyself to choose either melody or hush.

CXII
The Delights of a Yellow Warbler

Thyself to choose either melody or hush,
yellow warbler, bold beacon, away from shush-
the end of thy difficult days for thee
a blessing, refting away pain, would be.
How to accomplish such a feat isn't thy trill-
thou think on the closeness of minute thrill-
a drink in a puddle, a seed to snap up;
fellow warblers to sing to, in cottonwood to sup.
Thou in the tossing boughs of delight,
a meadow thy home, far from my sight,
what is thy opinion of the destruction of problems of this
world?
If thy tree blossomed fruit, thy joy unfurled?
Perhaps I'll translate the marigold one's thought,
the one that he'd have if he had been taught.

CXIII
Heaven for Hummingbirds

The thoughts that they'd have if they'd been taught,
that there is more beyond what here is wrought,
more that is pleasure, that is suffering's end;
the demons' works here they cannot defend.
For to try to comprehend such innocent,
as the hummingbird's wild frantic bent,
her heart beating one hundred times
being quick as heaven in earth's tedious clime,
yet and all the birds' every joy,
from time's first bird, created slow,
thus asking a spirit from heaven to be caught
in earth's moments of sunshine's plot,
is an unspeakable tale: ay to tell
of how is gifted sweet family by being's spell!

CXIV
Our Beloveds Will Accompany Us Into Heaven

Michael, the murmur or oak or walnut
outside, the lost warmth, the flowers' seeding,
tells me that soon the cold will wrap
around us, and snow will lay growth to sleep.
This waking, the awakening of the cold,
will burden the birds with their tiny bodies
and the deer in the hills will suffer hunger,
the cougars will continue their teeth tearing.
At least I can offer Thee this word packet,
giving the grace of thoughts heartfelt.
I pray for Thee in this autumn's leisure
that we will turn slowly into everlasting gold.
I speak of the angelic forms that we will find
when into heaven the angels pour pleasure.

Homage to a Lady
CXV
Arabian Girl

Oh the world is cruel to the harem girl
who within the walls that suppress her sits-
the men that lurk outside the door
have patient been to watch a lock flit
or costume sober or frown petulant-
their desire not fit to physical frame
then turns to dreams of onerous slant-
and creep then to capture more than girl's name-
they would grasp her days, her hours, of descant-
her fancy free chain to their taming
with what blows their minds vigilant
do subdue her domestic tranquility!, aiming
the girl to stifle with nary a grasp-
instead to thoughts of love kindly torture out her gasp!

CXVI
Japanese Geisha

Pale, of colors and layered as a flower's petals-
the geisha does with the artistry
of flute or swaying dance or song mettle
bring a chance of self-sufficiency
to the social jungle: in flower district
distinct from her past or future disentangled
she concentrates upon excellence beyond transfix
of sordid- she seeks sublime glimmered
of skin and cautious of pose wearing
kimono tied up like a present bejewled
in the independence of thought yet faring
on the gifts of patrons difficult gathered;
she stands on heels and grace admixed
to keep herself above the pleasure districts.

CXVII
Navajo Girl

Transplant not the piñon pine from habitat:
the Navajo girls let tend sheep in deserts
of colors saturated with slowness as a rug mat
woven with loops of skill like pottery, jewelry pleasant
to in the warmth of day like a shawl
covering the quiet, simply artisan craft-
they should not the native girls at all
from their home remove to city stagecraft
where is found criticism of mocking birds
of school children cruel of word and deed
chittering machinations of speed that disinterred
from their lives are as caveman brutes to happiness impede
as crudeness for brain is their way;
native girls live more civilized usually than they!

CXVIII
Indian Weaver

The vats of color- interpreted from jewels
(from how to celebrate color)- the dyes
that are used to make sari cloth in pools
in villages, and the intricate patterns- defy-
tie dyed diagonal block printed or two toned-
comprehension of how these village women's skill
is superior to modern fortune cost equipment wound
cloth- and no blonde goat haired saris (too volatile)
are made or mentioned- all hemp cotton and silk
a country that a success of home industry
has made has in its girls a milk
and honey land- of good karmic flurry
the women bejeweled in their native dress
weave the joy of India into goods of limpidness!

CXIX
Swiss Girl

Clamber before in a tangle of thought patterns-
goats or sheep you tend Swiss Alps girls-
you kill them not yet use their milk, wool- caverns
or crags not too troublesome when the sun impours
so gently in the landscape- here amongst wildflowers
the males yodel and the females listen soothed-
this is nature's cycle in sunlight- moonlight- hours
where man does work with naturalness as behooved
them- not to dominate or shun the chimerical
yet to allow the freshest aerosphere to inspire
freest thoughts- such as not to build at all
roads to load the landscape for ire
with heaps of houses; oh bright silver- waters-
you prefer pristine landscapes to stir sermoneer!

CXX
Balinese Dancer

Posturing as a gentle frangipani
that golden rests upon their youth dainty
a-tremble at the importance that a passer-by
notice the beauty; the Balinese dancers nigh
of Legong Kraton- the "Heavenly Dance
of the Divine Nymphs of the Palace"
immerse themselves in artistry
from a young age- not sophistry
yet the yearning to display a talent
thus to be considered a part not supereminent:
what is fraudulent is the imitation
of royalty- personages in gold brocade configuration
find that not a palace a feint procures-
not a real crown is a theatrical gown.

CXXI
Guatemalan Weaver

The weavers of history so remote from
the Guatemalan weavers- girls whom
in front of houses sit with looms tied to trees
weaving multicolors of patterns strict not portentiously-
oh weavers you must memorize with such skill
from the thousands of variations minute and versatile
to earn a life in which you can survive
pray for the weaver that she will thrive!
Life's game is harsh yet she still works
outlasting civilizations- Mayan- with fancywork
that patiently- tediously- is learned
from the teachers whom do not spurn
a young girl of silk skein hair- shy of smile-
pondering nature and how best to capture its style-

CXXII
Mexican Silver Worker

To produce works of beauty you craft
oh Mexican silver workers the ingots culled
from dark places inside the earth nearby your village- drift
to you the toughness of a life with work not dull
as a mind would wish- with imagination's plan
you created enduring works of extreme beauty- mention
of needing to perfect the work in this Aztec land-
the pieces often more Pre-Columbian than Christian
era of motif- the masters shouldn't too much a burden
place upon the workers who had learnt
from Europeans their craft- predecessors
whom worked gold and silver for kings were not
about to stop their artistry- the work always newer
to those artisans whom go into the future years.

CXXIII
Amish Girl

You that quilt, that wear a dress and bonnet-
of the Dutch settlers earlier upon this continent-
old fashioned Amish girl apart from moderninity
walking and working without machine of industry-
refusing morals of the slack twentieth century
(whose spirals jetted downwards to lives sturdy
of city life a rampant zoo)- Nay!
The individual collective of museum way?
The stricture of conservativism that refuses to change?
Whatever generating forces solidified unprofaned
some might say to be analyzed by crew
of historian or sociologist to reconstrue-
I deem the desire for a country life
is admirable enough to elude any hype.

CXXIV
Bedouin Girl

I do not share a passion for wanderlust
with the Bedouin women who with khol eyes
smouldering in desert nights stitch tent from dust
of camel hair woven- they must create a house sized
from antiquity each time they travel-
their men leave stones in desert tracks
to guide their return- ordeal or surreal
I cannot say- not liking either crammed together- in cloth
dressed from head to toe and veiled from sun and grit
yet they can read the stars for direction
living in that suspended time of: prerequisite
not being lonely in dunes of insurrection:
not caravan just travelers of two
the wife and husband are the escaping crew.

CXXV
African Girl

An African sunset: and the Zulu girl
has all day in the forest spent
gathering wood and water from spring that began
in pre-historic reeds of antique rustling bent
and carrying these on her head,
to her home to cook the meal
in ashes with companions to be fed
that collective they can fend the wild steal
off of animals: this is after the progress of years
what the tribe has achieved; a civility
wresting from wilderness a life to inhere
as free women not caught in slavery
and true that the modern girl from a slave
lives as distant in being than a lady from her maids.

CXXVI
Chinese Acrobat

You tumble and clamber more gracefully
than any pet capuchin- oh acrobats of China
with costumes of brilliant colors like evening dress unruly
of headpiece like opera hats- a sign of
your ability to balance anywhere even on stacks
of chairs or in pyramids of humans-
this entertainment traps masses in drawback
of defiance of the real with fuming
unreal combinations of posturing- as odd
to confuse a peasant with a queen!
Yet not to be of the exhibition overawed
or driven to tears- for here comes the scene
of shaggy dragon dressed in gold-
not to fear with a happy dragon so bold!

At first the mind begins to spin of thought
insubstantial, gossamer and unfalse
potential packed as days' waltz,
and what a fresh mind finds is heresy wrought-
the self to be an emperor of language
vaulting the perfection higher than scholars thought
before to strict adhesion of control of ego fought;
what unsubstantial freedoms of pupilage
that the being believing in its potency
can fashion such a whirl above gravitation?
And can flaunt strictures of subordination-
flitting past the bindings of energy?-
How- can I remain upwards of sin
when the gravitation is mastered from within?

CXXVIII
Love Paradox

Capture my love! Is that what dost thou say?
Then capture the moon within a net
and swing it closer into the earth- set-
(it wanders farther eventually on its own way-)
tell the sea to stop its ebb and flow
and only wait azure in one place-
tell the trees to towards the ground race
instead of towards the sky steer their prow-
name the flowers for colorlessness
all pallid thin and wilting in the sun-
tell them not to enjoy the daylight's hum-
to night instead all adore in willingness-
Oh! Nature does to withstand force pray-
lest gravity high tide willow and night blooms betray-

CXXIX
Mind Renewal

Is the world of accomplishment a mountain range worn
from time- in ages it rubbles away with weather
slowly from Himaleyah to a hill shorn?
Until all that is left is in smooth altogether?
Or if the works an ocean does purr
hiding in deeps secret lives more odd
than is spoken aloud, rising chronicler
then retreating in difficult patters to quieter laud:
the intervals to measure are separate-
for one is declension to a mildness
and one an every year's interpolate
flow: methinks the sour old vexatiousness
renewed by new lives into youth
do prove that the mind is a sea is truth.

CXXX
Individual Will

The individual will is contained in a frame
of flesh that stands and walks in its own energy:
the commanding will connected is to a sea synergy
like swarm in hive of city names-
how one can be through the stubbornness
of thought and deed to be itself
and not join in the commonwealth
of behavior patterns- desire to suppress
and the machine of fate to transgress
through exigency of the filaments of good
ley lines of help and in daylight understood
to stave off that duty's burden- limpidness
however when the light entangles
in dusk- dispersed- is an ancient wrangle.

CXXXI
Disobedience

Dream robber- maraud dost thou my time
an engulfment then of sweet territory
my midnight- morning- matin- narratory-
of whisper to my thought- no pastime
allurant so chimes to the inwards heart
of with what it ought to sympathize-
bolder transport than pure frenzy and sighs-
for this is plot and care to desire impart
and to grow within my inward frame
obedience to that gentility's night
where passion rests in survival not sylvanite
yet yielding- to the power of the name-
how seek to topple thou the guileless fortress of me
so quickly with a mere mental synergy?

CXXXII
Conquer Passion

I tell the news- I tell it mild-
careful- love- what thou dost choose
of amorousness as an armor- to infuse
with thy capability into this self beguiled-
the youth of my self dost thee implore
to be cautious- when thy thought dost run
so that it does not outshine that sun
whereby I am nourished- be sparse of desire therefore-
and hold thy temptation of begging more
than what is outlined in necessity-
give me in my own mind a locality
to be- serene- and to transcend conquerer
of doubt- to love is not a game:
nor a knot to unravel wildness and me entame!

CXXXIII
Tame Thyself!

To speak to the maddened by power, by lust
is to lilt a phrase of a foreign tongue
that they do not comprehend the meaning among
the syllables: if I speak: thy self distrust
and wary of thy wantonness become
not to fathoms of disgrace adhere
to the corps of battlement be mutineer
bold as brigand to thyself fight benumbed
to thy orders: still that urgency
of hazardous project: a distance from turbulence
of lust's fulfillment thus beg I overpowered in self-defense
my cautious plea: not recklessly
our futures beshrew with a shadow-
thy self comprehend to be beyond a slavish tableau!

CXXXIV
Appeal to Reason

I must tell reason to rein in passion astray!
As a Christian soul I must to temptation
a frown fling- a cajole of calculation
to best tip sin from off its expose
of more gossiped fodder of incantation
and quietly inside feel free of a spell-
how much longer will not be my task to tell-
of a breath of liberal thought the literalization
so the soul has waves as of air
circumnambulating to the respective poles
of perfection and of desire- just a toll
of youth is my scattered walkabout- beware-
thy blithe passion also quell- hold-
keep thyself not synonymous with any impetus
uncontrolled-

CXXXV
Love's Lessons

He teaches me to love linear things
like the lineaments of his thoughtful hands;
his mind's tendrils that to me cling
like a fervent intricacy of demand;
once I was a lark on wing above
his gentle falconry occasions
when he to my heart dove
with all his urgency of command station-
I knew myself not to be his houri slave
with eyes aglow for the light inner lit
my own light than his more ancient- stave
and battlements my forage of every day's wit-
oh I would that my past I had clung to
that a weakened daisy I not be plucked so.

CXXXVI
Love In the World

I care not a fig if the world's mating's amiss
now half in winter and half in summer
half in midnight and half in noon
half sight the sun and half peer at moon!
Not less could I sorrow that the men
are half and more of the dreaded plight;
so cruel and so *demanding* in attacks of flight!
Few of them matter to the base of me!
And half is water and half is air!
Whereof is the cleansing here?
Mastery- misery- fling maddened away!
Shout at the dawn of the day!
For know I at least- this: that their attempts
to bring songs here are pure resilience!

CXXXVII
Witholding Desire

Beings of such multitude: only here
minds a-thirst for desire; should not be quenched!
Hearts asking that a portions them drench
in love: must be analyzed if any particles leer!
Then guess that what I love is song
and turning away from dearth's drown
in bundles of buckets of lusting strangeness worn!
Instead I find a future formed- long-
of what I pray is my own willpower
to fight that scourge of subduing
the courage to acceptance then ruing-
oh *when* will I ever become apart from weakness' dower?
Part in wondering form I the hours-
what- the birds' songs mean for flowers!

CXXXVIII
Limiting Loves

What concerns me is not that which
my unconsciousness is attacked by:
not the repetitive torture to swimmingly move
of helpless- constant- control- of consciousness:
that the males of creation are- except for some-
not more than sinners- fallen for fun-
that the ancient friends left are few
that this world produced many foes new-
not to fret like a loud chord
that "I am one- and they are forty- four!"
For the "remedy of the malady" quickly I encounter;
the proper mixture of realize- persevere!
As evolution from kindness can also assuage
psychic primitiveness after the lessons of ages!

CXXXIX
Friendship and Passion

To write when the emotion wrings my being
(Is it mine? That swush of energy within?)
simple- spells the words can creep away from din:
then is the sin of passion poems freeing?
Does the intricacy of the intimate
not the male twine into a constancy?
Of intuition- does it not encounter the destiny
that friendship is the lasting- not the innocent?
With the dawn's each privacy
becomes more tenuous as if of dew
the lie (replaced with truth that we can select our own- new-
society that urges involvement so little of piracy)-
and the depths of to desire to transmute
towards Krishna is the answer they say suits.

CXL
Hurrah For Angels!

At last I hope I have a true one found-
of the many that do linger in time
there are paucity of beings of eternal mind-
then give this one a golden crown!
If towards the celebrated we spy
(those that dance upon the stage
that pass through- importance- not betrayed-
we find few that are real or high)-
so if I pluck from the dust gold sifter
after impossible to tell years of living wise-
a few of gold to turn to wear- sigh-
then that is preferable to endless drifters!
So angels baffle with this news:
perhaps I can learn to both fight and use!

Futurenote Sonnets
CXLI

Now that the drug of you is calmed
with the drug of sleep I can think
back to the time of our conversation drink
of reality not superficial and not becalmed
to stasis and wonder about that plot
to weaken desire for intellectuality
perhaps because they know not (pity)
that the two mixed are sharper- (gavotte
to two step)- of pleasure that begins in mind
anyway and from thence is sent hither
to duties of what consequence could I encounter
were I older: now I can only self-scorn find
upon my lack of experience-
I knew not to check completely my etheriance!

To say that the personality of those other girls
is like mine is as much as to presuppose
a cosine wave flipping up to ecstatic whirls
then a distance away from foes
next the loops of fluttering cerulean
unlike any stricture, the wish for plays
more than one for every hundred apogean:
or to state perhaps that the sky blue stays
and this is me; that azure unobtainable
when the colors tinting are gold, silver, maize-
rose and purple- mauve and pearl grey- fabled-
just admit the multiplicity of my ways
and the hauteur that others choose-
I now in variance more surprise of news.

CXLIII
Notice of Paradigm Shift

I thank God for his splendrous ways-
found in the song of Nature's arrays-
I thank him for his loving commands
that delineate for me the outlines of his plans-
I think of God in Sunshine-
when the sky is Krishna blue-
I achieve a symbiosis occasional
with the energy that all plants grows-
the Joy! Is to be rooted temporarily in place
where God's brilliance can be sought
merely by breathing in t air
or watching sweet rain- believe!
I Believe- all Nature at times
refers to how to praise God's name!

CXLIV
Nature the Balancer

There is Goodness even in the hell
of materiality's gravity components-
even in a World of society
that chooses wickedness- defiancy-
even here the Springtime yearly arrives
the Songs of Sparrows the Blossoms strewn liberally-
the shining daytime Light
and the gentle zephyrs- twinkling the stars at night-
even those are given to the wicked people
despite their defeat of themselves
their pleasures- futures- and of their lives:
after years of working to enact a grime
of grumpiness and dirty soot upon the landscape-
yet the winds and rains still cleanse the sky.

CXLV
Landscapes are not Created to be Destroyed

How much intelligence there is in the World!
Found in nature- every Being including of leaf or fur-
the Trees know how to Loftily Lift
their green for Oxygen production's gift-
the Flora find how to imbue
themselves of gorgeous Form and hue-
and the fauna can find themselves
steadily of continuance- even in winter's chilled ice shelves-
and the people too are smart
in certain material creating works to start;
somewhat of knowledge has built up their race
for Aartworks sciences and technology's pace-
yet the people's intelligence a certain aspect lacks-
respect for Nature's wisdom of leaving Wilderness in fact-

CXLVI
A Meditation Upon What the Rain Teaches

I love the days when there is a rain
and the landscape wears a silver hat of clouds-
I like the energy and the serenity
like that life of a high-born house
where the hush and tick tock of the clock
are the only sounds to hear of-
I could wander in the meadows for a thrill
were it not for the ant heap humans
whom have built up their town-
with resonance of an energy not that previous found-
Every place should be a Nature Preserve
with only enough humans not to deface
the artistic inclinations of natural grace,
dirt paths the only roads.

CXLVII
The Swift

All except the air is scorned by the swift,
rejecting the ground with her white throat a-quiver;
coaxing the wind from the morning adrift,
through the wind of her own she shivers.
Tossing the sky between his skillful hands,
peregrine now passes in questing fury
thrusting his way like a fiery demand
on the sky of the morning, now blurry.
Suddenly, on wing, their paths assemble
quick talons grasp for the delicate upwings.
Coalescing in a primitive heat, they dissemble
not, in the final apotheosis of plundering.
Caught by their nature, into this gyre,
the pursuer and prey both turn to fire.

anhuac- the plateau of central Mexico, including Mexico city, the centre of aztecs' civilization

antediluvial- that which disappeared before the mythical flood of the Bible; what happened a very long time ago

apocryphal- (nice); not canonical, or officially accepted; beyond means of deciphering authority definitively

apogean- the place where a heavenly body is farthest from the sun; could be of thought too

aarcturus- the fourth biggest star of the visible night sky and of the milky way galaxy; connotes "bear"

armillary sphere- an arrangement of rings together to show the orbits of the planets and with the sun in centre

ashoka- the third bc Indian maharaja of Maduryan Dynasty who ruled all the Indian subcontinent and who was tolerant of various minority religions

astrolabe- an instrument for calculating the altitude of sun or stars at sea

Atacama- a province of Chile, with a famous desert

attar of roses- a perfume made from roses associated with the exotical of the orient

attars- from flowers that are perfumed; floral prettiness

Baal- various local nature deities worshipped by ancient Semitic peoples; "I will take the name of Baal out of your mouths" said Jehoveh

backstaff- an instrument for measuring the altitude of heavenly deities

Bedouin- an Arab of the desert in Asia or Africa; a nomad; a wanderer of the desert, and thus exotic

benison- a blessing spoken by a person; a smooth unworried word

blazoning- from emblazon, with a hint of heraldic displays of color and verve

buffet- (verb); to fight, to struggle, as to more despite storm

Caryan Kingdom- a kingdom in South America of in the now Ecuadorian region

Caroline Hershel- 19th century British astronomer the sister of the famous Frederich Hershel, who discovered a comet

Catherine de Medici- 16th century Italian princess sent to become a queen in France- Lorenzo de Medici's daughter

cavalier- either a knight, a courtly gentleman, a man escorting a lady, or a gallant

chastening- to kindly and sweetly lead towards, moral improvement with coaxing and kindness and dulcet behaviour, or ought to be thus

chimerical- pertaining to the culture of a chimera, thus, of fantasy; shifting, imaginary

Christina- Queen Christina of Sweden; a 17th century intellectual; beautiful and made queen at age 6

chthonic- that which dwells in the earth or in the underworld of the earth; original to a place

circumambulating- a walking meditation used by many religions usually around a site sacred to their religion

circumscribed- to set a parameter of definition which helps in the comprehension; yet; there could be more awe in heaven and earth than that

Constable- 18th to 19th English landscape painter whose paintings evoke calmness happiness and peace

cosmic dust- matter in fine particles falling in from space

cosmotherium- an antique model that demonstrated the orbits around the sun of planets, and each could be positioned variously

corolla- a ring or a halo around something; from the Latin word crown; also botanical

cosine wave- a cosine is one measure of a right triangle's angles

crepuscular- pertaining to twilight, with a shadowy umbra about it, (purpleish)

crystalline sphere- in ancient astronomy, spheres that held the stars and sun in them, and turned to form the night sky *cuzco-* a city in Southern Peru founded by the Capacs and made a capital of an Incan empire

dayspring- the beginning of day, as it starts from the horizon and shifts up into sky

Deir-el-Bahri- a complex of mortuary temples and tombs in Thebes, Egypt

Diane of Potiers- 16th century French duchess of Henry II of France

disinterred- not only to bring forth from the grave; also, to bring from obscurity into view

distillation- the purification and refinement of a liquid; an essence of delight given

ecliptic- the circle formed by the earth's orbit passing through the celestial sphere; the annual path of the sun in the heavens

elegiast- one who writes elegies of meditation upon sweet lamentation

Empress Jingo- the 2nd – 3rd century ad legendary Japanese empress supposedly who invaded Korea successfully

England's yule- the winter solstice of the 21st or 22nd of December now associated with the Christian holiday of Jesus' birthday

equinoctical sphere- a circle through the poles that divides the earth

etheriance- that which is heavenly; atmospheric of pleasing aura; tending to escape earth gravity in transcendence

fallow- uncultivated land, left to its own devices

ferret- (verb); to search out or to hunt for, knowledge that is obscure

fiat- a decree by a person in authority, who has panache verve and style

fife- a small high pitched flute used in mountainous or mythical settings

frangipani- a type of tropical flower tree or shrub utilized by many peoples for ornamental decoration

Frederick of Prussia- 18th century Prussian king quite fond of war *galleon-* a large sailing ship used by Spaniards for commerce and in quarrels with other peoples

genesis- (biblical verb); originating, beginning, creating

glens- a secluded summer valley to be thought of poetically and not aesthetically

gnomic- a vast wisdom in few words

Golden Horde- a Mongolian army that swept over Eastern Europe in the 13th century and who established a suzerain in Russia

Gupta- Chandra Gupta Maurya is the 4th to 5th century bc founder of the Mauryan Empire in India

hairy star- (comet); from the greek for long haired, referring in personification and in anthromorphism to the characteristics of a comet

halcyon- when a fabled bird calms the wind and wave, it is called a halcyon and a day thus perfect is that

Hari- a name for Krishna, meaning, praise, in Sanskrit

Hatshepsu- 15th century bc pharaoh, very rare because a female

Henry II- 18th century king of France who regained Calais from the English and who had many romantic complications

heresy- thinking for one's self instead of orthodoxy (mob rule)

Himaleyah- a mountain range with including a mountain before thought to be the world's tallest

Huanicanacapac- 16th century Incan emperor

inflection- modulation of something, or a motion in a curve, or vibration in words

insurrection- a rising of rebellion against a tyrranous authority; nowadays, a social gathering such as a poetry reading

interpolate- to add new material, or, between two poles

Jain- a very ancient religion of India, which emphasized asceticism, reverence for all life, and respect for wisdom

Justinian- 5th to 6th century ad Byzantine emperor who kept the Persians away and who codified laws *ka'bah-* a building in the great mosque at mecca enclosing a stone that muslims face when praying and to which good muslims must make a pilgrimage

Kano- an ancient city in Nigeria

Katsana- an ancient city in Nigeria

Kazanlik- a famous town in central Bulgaria for its beautiful expensive roses overtaken by the Ottoman Turks in the 14th century

khol- a type of Egyptian makeup to render the person with alluring eyes

khorten- a type of Tibetan prayer wheel containing parchment on which prayers are written

King Mu- 7th century Korean king who built a famous temple complex

kiptchack khanate- the territory or realm ruled by the Mongols

knoll- a small hill or elevation, that sounds celtic and is indeed forlorn

Krishna- an incarnation of the god Vishnu, whose adventures were told in the Bhagavad-Gita

lapis- a type of semiprecious gem of azure that has a tranquility

lathe- that which shapes wood into useful or decorative items, to smooth it towards the beautiful

leaven- to transform into that which is lighter and higher

lexicon- a dictionary of a particular vocabulary associated with a field of knowledge; sounds quite precise and perhaps prim and proper

lieu- in place of, instead

logos- the word word as representing Jesus as the patron of books

Lorenzo de Medici- 15th century prince the ruler of Florence a patron of the Renaissance

madurya- refers to the complete beauty and sweetness of Krishna; it means that which is sweetest

malingerers- taken to mean the feeling of loneliness from evil that should not linger *maraud-* to move in quest of plunder; poetically, to attempt to steal the emotions

Maria Teresa- 18th century Austrian empress of Hapsburg family who did not rescue her daughter Marie Antoinette

matin- pertaining to the morning; worship, prayers, songs in the early hours; a song of the morning

Mauryans- 4th – 2nd century bc empire and power or empire in India

maverick- one who departs from customs or beliefs of his group, named after a texas ranger who would not brand his cattle

median- in mathematics, a middle value of a set of values

mellifluent- sweet sounding; flowing like honey

merkhabah- from the Hebrew for chariot, used by Ezekiel to denote an early ufo experience

metamorphosis- the achievement of transformation into a higher type of being of consciousness through self-will

Ming- a Chinese dynasty, 14th to 17th centuries in which the arts were highly developed to an excellence

Miruk- (Korean); another name for Buddha Maitreya, the Buddha of the future

mutineer- one who resists authority

Nezanhualcoyotl- (tasting coyote); 15th century precolombian musician and philosopher architect and ruler of Texoco

noblesse oblige- taken to mean, the priviledge and superior benefits of the aristocracy

Northumbria- a province of England, northern, with moors

Novgorod- a province of Russia also a city in Russia

obeisance- a graceful bow of respect seeming to conjure images of salaaming servants ?

Ogodon Khan- 13th century Mongolian leader second in power after Ghengis Khan

omega- the last letter of the Greek alphabet, raised in emotive capability by the book of Revelation to indicate eschatology *opulency-* the ostentation of style of fabulous wealth, which can be of the mind

orison- a prayer or supplication perhaps sounding gothic

Ottoman- pertaining to the Turkish dynasty set up by Ossman (Othman) in 1300

padma chakra- with the literal interpretation of lotus wheel in Sanskrit, an early idea of a type of ufo from ancient Indian texts

parure- a set of jewels or ornaments, which can be a matched set of necklaces, bracelets, earrings

pelt- used to indicate to form of a being

peridezea- a Persian word meaning walled garden, the source for English paradise

perpetual calendar- a calendar that demonstrates many years, often in advance

plumb bob- that which helps the plumb line determine perpendicularity

Potala- the palace of the Dalai Lama in Tibet, that overlooks the city

"Pro reginae vitam et sanguinam consecramus"- for the queen we consecrate our lives and our blood; latin

pthonic- refers to the priestess of Delphi; the Pythia becomes Apollo who slew a giant python at that place

quadrant- the one of a circle containing ninety degrees angles; a section of space

Radha- Radha and Krishna are known as the all-attractive couple

reconstrue- to rethink, reimagine, perhaps to improve…

roseate- deep pink and roses colored and blush and promising

sacrosanct- that which is exceptionally sacred and not to be violated; protected of spiritual forces

Saracens- nomadic tribes on the Syrian borders of the Roman empire, moslem with respect to the crusades

Saurriya Amira- 16th century queen of Zaria who gives a name to Zazzu province of modern Nigeria *satyr-*   a sylvan creature of classical mythology, often clever and wry

Savonorola-   15th century Italian religious and political reformer who preached again and again against corruption

scimitars-   an oriental sword curved like a crescent

scion-   from plant material to make new life asexually

sequestering-   the act of secluding and privatizing an individual, in order to influence them more hypnotically (?)

sheol-   the Hebrew abode of departed spirits

sostitial colure-   two times of the year when the sun is at the greatest distance from the equator; a colure is two circles of celestial sphere intersecting each other at right angles of the celestial poles

Srong-lotsam-sgampo-   7th century important Tibetan king

substratum-   a foundational layer which supports the rest

Sumanguru-   15th century West African ruler, who conquered small Sudanese states and the capital of the Ghanan empire

Sundiata Keita-   13th century founder of the Mali empire celebrated by the Malinke people

suzerain-   a feudal lord or baron or a ruler who influences an adjunct state (such as sitting next to the king at a dinner party)

sylvanite-   inhabiting the woods, as sylphs; the words slips away

synechdoche-   that which imagines the whole as a part or a part as a whole

synergy-   that which works in tandem gracefully to combine functioning

tacitly-   implied though not directly; implied with tact

tar-   a seaman; living in boats; a sea-drenched word

taro-   an edible plant of the tropics

telesis-   progress intelligently planned, related to telos, an aim or a goal

terribilitas-   (nature); reference to the power of nature to awe (not negative)

Theodora-   6th century ad Byzantine empress

Titans'- landless beings of giant age who wished to overthrow gods

titularity- holding of a title

transfixing- to render immoveable with awe, as gods know how to do

transmute- to evolve from one form to a higher, more delicate one

tremolo- a tremulous, vibrating effect of instruments and varies; awakening of emotion

triune- three in one; what else is triune besides Trinity?

troth- a pledge

trounce- to defeat, complete, impressively

trousseau- the collections of personal effects which a bride to be assembles in anticipation; (?antiquated?)

unified field- a quaint fiction of Einstein, that indicates the unification of theories into one, as if they were rental properties

vestal virgin- one of the maidens consecrated to keeping the sacred fire of Vesta burning; (chaste)

vile- a high minded way to react to the annoyances of evil is to call them vile, particularly if they are good looking

Yeshua- Jesus' Hebrew name

yen- urge; an intense desire, longing, for something not quite specified and a little vague

yin- the female, passive force in nature, thought to be either opposite or complementary to yang

Zion- so many connotations are pertinent; one supercedes; the lofty place where Jesus lives and where the saints gather to praise him

Zulu- southeastern African tribe quite self promoting of culture

(blessings upon freedoms of thought)

CPSIA information can be obtained at www.ICGtesting.com
Printed in the USA
BVOW011127030812

297006BV00001B/1/P